BISON

Dylanna Press

Copyright © 2025 by Dylanna Press
Author: Tyler Grady

All rights reserved. No part of this publication may be reproduced, stored in a retrieval system, or transmitted by any means, including electronic, mechanical, photocopying, or otherwise, without prior written permission of the publisher.

Although the publisher has taken all reasonable care in the preparation of this book, we make no warranty about the accuracy or completeness of its content and, to the maximum extent permitted, disclaim all liability arising from its use.

Trademarks: Dylanna Press is a registered trademark of Dylanna Publishing, Inc. and may not be used without written permission.

ISBN: 978-1647904265 (pb); 978-1647904500 (hc)
Publisher: Dylanna Publishing, Inc.
First Edition: 2025

10 9 8 7 6 5 4 3 2 1

For information about special discounts for bulk purchases, please contact:

orders@dylannpublishing.com
Dylanna Publishing, Inc.
www.dylannapublishing.com

Contents

Meet the American Bison — 7
Built for the Prairie — 8
Life on the Grasslands — 11
Adapted for the Prairie — 12
What Do Bison Eat? — 15
Life in the Herd — 16
On the Move — 18
A Day in the Life — 20
Mating and Birth — 23
Growing Up Bison — 24
Bison and Their Ecosystem — 27
Natural Predators — 28
Challenges and Threats — 31
Life Span and Population — 32
Conclusion — 35
Test Your Bison Knowledge! — 36
STEM Challenge: Think Like a Scientist! — 37
Word Search — 38
Glossary — 39
Resources and References — 40
Index — 41

Fun Fact: In 2016, President Obama signed a law making the American bison the official national mammal of the United States—joining the bald eagle as a symbol of America!

Meet the American Bison

RUMBLE! RUMBLE! RUMBLE! The ground shakes beneath thousands of hooves as a massive herd thunders across the open prairie. Dust clouds rise into the sky like brown smoke signals. These shaggy giants—each one bigger than a refrigerator—move together in a river of fur and muscle that stretches as far as you can see. Welcome to the world of the American bison!

These powerful mammals are the largest land animals in North America. With their enormous heads, high shoulder humps, and thick, shaggy coats, bison look like they walked straight out of the Ice Age—and they basically did! Their ancestors roamed this continent alongside woolly mammoths and saber-toothed cats.

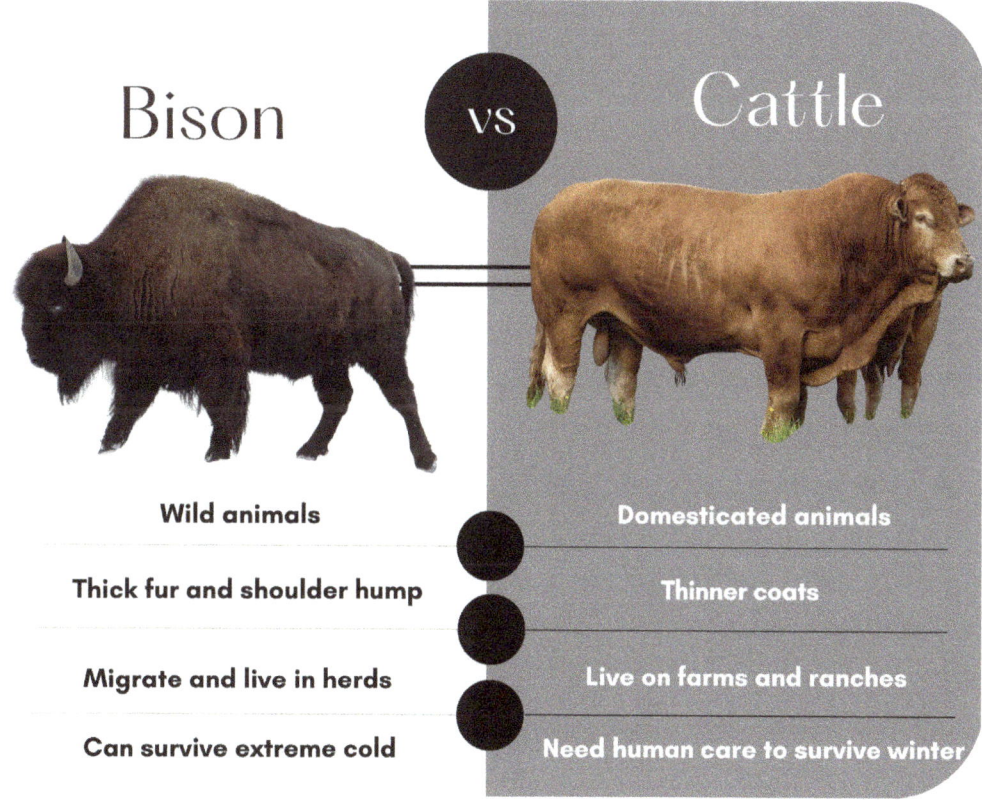

Bison once numbered in the tens of millions, with herds so vast they could take days to pass by a single spot. Tragically, by the late 1800s, hunters had reduced their numbers to fewer than 1,000 animals. Today, thanks to dedicated conservation efforts, bison are making a comeback. You can find wild herds in national parks, preserves, and tribal lands across the United States and Canada.

Their scientific name is *Bison bison*—yes, bison is so nice they named it twice! They belong to the Bovidae family along with cattle, goats, and sheep. And while many people call them "buffalo," that's actually a nickname. True buffalo live in Africa and Asia. These North American giants are 100% bison—and 100% amazing.

Built for the Prairie

Bison are some of the most imposing animals in North America. Despite their bulky appearance, bison are incredibly strong and agile. An adult bison standing on all fours is about as tall as a refrigerator (5 to 6 feet [150 to 180 cm] at the shoulder) and up to 12 feet (365 cm) in length. Males, known as bulls, are much larger than females, weighing 1,000 to 2,200 pounds (450 to 1,000 kg), while females, or cows, typically weigh 790 to 1,200 pounds (360 to 540 kg).

One of their most distinctive features is the prominent shoulder hump, created by powerful muscles supported by long vertebrae. This hump, along with their massive head and thick neck, helps bison plow through deep snow in winter as they search for buried grasses.

Both male and female bison have curved, sharp horns that grow throughout their lives. These horns are used for defense against predators and during dominance battles between bulls. Their thick, woolly coats that insulate them from extreme temperatures, shedding in the summer to keep cool and regrowing in winter to endure freezing conditions.

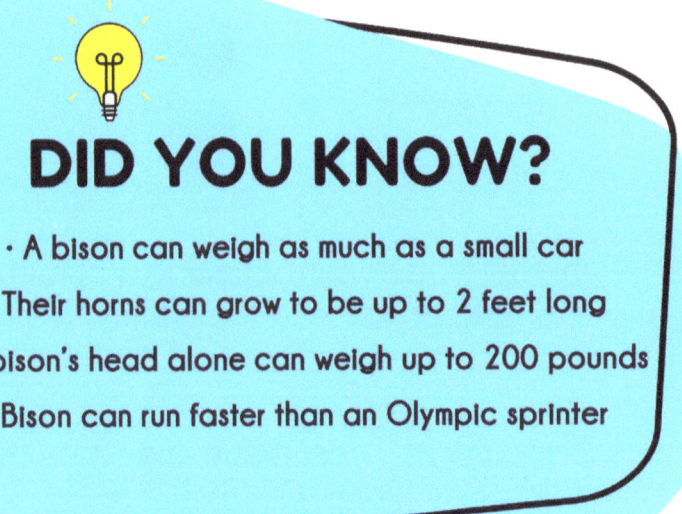

DID YOU KNOW?
- A bison can weigh as much as a small car
- Their horns can grow to be up to 2 feet long
- A bison's head alone can weigh up to 200 pounds
- Bison can run faster than an Olympic sprinter

Fun Fact: Despite their size, bison can jump fences 6 feet (1.8 meters) high.

Fun Fact: Bison don't walk around blizzards—they walk straight into them! Facing the storm lets them get through bad weather faster than animals that try to run away from it.

Life on the Grasslands

Bison are animals of wide-open spaces, perfectly adapted to life on the great grasslands of North America. Historically, they ranged across most of the continent, from Alaska's tundra to Mexico's grasslands, and from the eastern woodlands to the western mountains.

Their primary habitat is prairie grassland, with its vast, open landscapes and mix of grasses. Unlike many large mammals that require forests or dense vegetation for protection, bison thrive in open landscapes where they can see potential predators from a distance and move freely in herds.

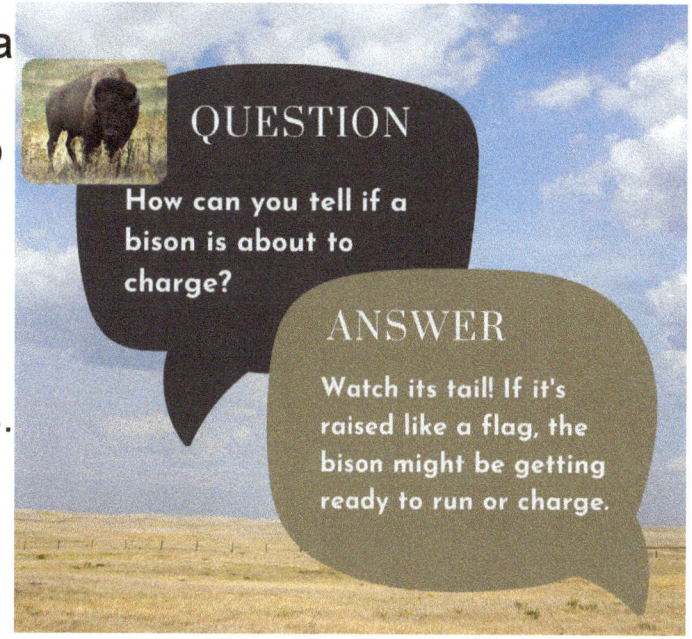

QUESTION
How can you tell if a bison is about to charge?

ANSWER
Watch its tail! If it's raised like a flag, the bison might be getting ready to run or charge.

Bison have adapted to survive in some of North America's most extreme environments. They can endure winter temperatures far below freezing and summer heat well over 100°F (38°C). Their natural habitats experience everything from drought and prairie fires to blizzards and floods. Rather than seeking permanent shelter, bison move with the seasons, following the growth of fresh grass and avoiding the worst weather conditions.

Despite their massive size, bison are incredibly fast and agile. They can run at speeds up to 35 miles per hour (56 kilometers per hour)—faster than a racehorse! Their specially adapted hooves provide excellent traction in mud or snow, and they use these strong hooves to dig through deep snow to reach grass in winter.

Adapted for the Prairie

Bison have developed several physical **adaptations** that make them perfectly suited to their prairie habitat.

- **Massive Head and Neck:** Bison have incredibly strong neck muscles and a large, heavy head that acts like a snowplow in winter. This powerful combination allows them to sweep their head from side to side through deep snow to reach the grass below.

- **Specialized Digestive System:** Bison have a complex four-chambered stomach that helps them extract maximum nutrition from tough prairie grasses. Like other grazing animals, they can regurgitate partially digested food (called cud) to chew it again, getting more nutrients from each mouthful.

- **Weather-Ready Coat:** Their thick fur has multiple layers—a dense, woolly undercoat covered by longer guard hairs. In winter, this coat can be up to 2 inches (5 cm) thick, providing excellent insulation against frigid temperatures. They shed this heavy coat in spring when warmer weather arrives.

- **Powerful Shoulder Hump:** The distinctive hump on a bison's shoulders isn't filled with fat—it's solid muscle supported by long vertebrae. These powerful muscles help bison use their head as a tool for moving snow and for self-defense.

- **All-Terrain Hooves:** Their split hooves are wide and hard for better stability in mud or snow, while also helping them run at high speeds across rough terrain. Bison can sprint at speeds up to 35 miles per hour (56 kilometers per hour) and jump over obstacles up to 6 feet (1.8 meters) high.

- **Thick Hide:** Their thick, dark skin protects them from intense summer sun and biting insects. They also take dust baths, rolling in dry soil to create an extra layer of protection against pests.

- **Enhanced Senses:** Bison have excellent hearing and sense of smell, helping them detect predators from great distances. Their eyes are positioned on the sides of their head, giving them a wide field of vision to spot danger while grazing.

These adaptations make bison uniquely suited to the expansive grasslands of North America.

Fun Fact: Bison are nature's lawnmowers! A single bison can munch through enough grass to fill about 300 cereal bowls every day.

What Do Bison Eat?

Bison are grazers, feeding mainly on different types of prairie grasses. Unlike other **herbivores** such as deer and elk that eat leaves and twigs from trees and bushes, bison are specially adapted to thrive on the tough grasses of the open plains.

These massive animals adjust their diet with the seasons. In spring and summer, they select tender new growth rich in nutrients. During fall, they feed more heavily on taller grasses that have gone to seed. Even in winter, they can find and digest dried grasses that other animals can't eat.

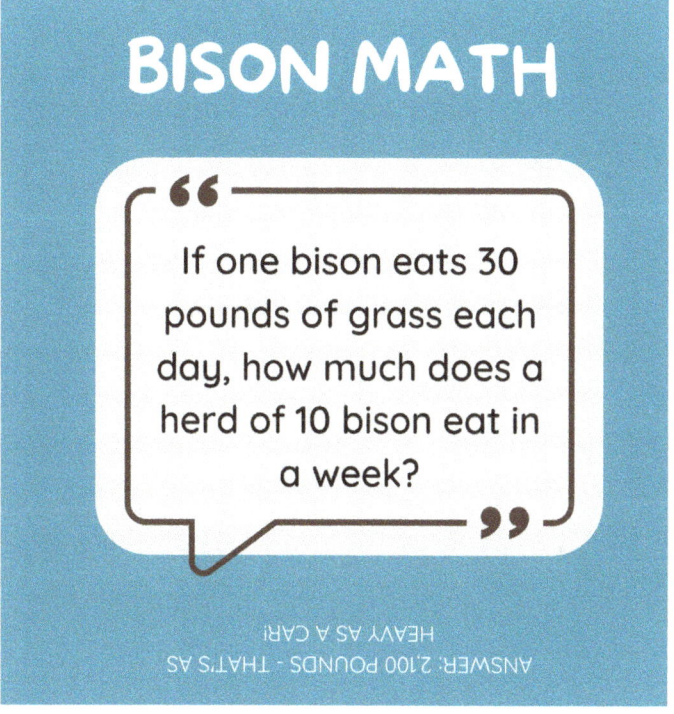

BISON MATH

"If one bison eats 30 pounds of grass each day, how much does a herd of 10 bison eat in a week?"

ANSWER: 2,100 POUNDS - THAT'S AS HEAVY AS A CAR!

A single adult bison can consume up to 30 pounds (14 kg) of grass per day. They prefer to graze in the cooler morning and evening hours, especially during hot summers. Bison need to drink frequently, consuming up to 10 gallons (38 liters) of water per day. During winter, they often eat snow to meet their water needs. Herds typically stay near reliable water sources, especially during hot summer months.

Like other grazing animals, bison have a specialized digestive system that helps them get the most nutrition from grass. They have a large stomach divided into four chambers, filled with helpful bacteria that break down tough plant fibers. Bison will often **regurgitate** partially digested grass (called cud) to chew it again, helping them get more nutrients from their food.

Life in the Herd

Bison are social animals that live in herds. Unlike many other large mammals that form small family groups, bison herds can include hundreds of individuals. For most of the year, these herds consist of females (called cows), their calves, and young males. Adult males (bulls) usually live in smaller bachelor groups or sometimes alone, joining the larger herds during mating season.

The size of bison herds changes with the seasons. In summer, herds can grow very large as they move across the grasslands together. During winter, these large herds often break into smaller groups to better survive the harsh conditions and find enough food.

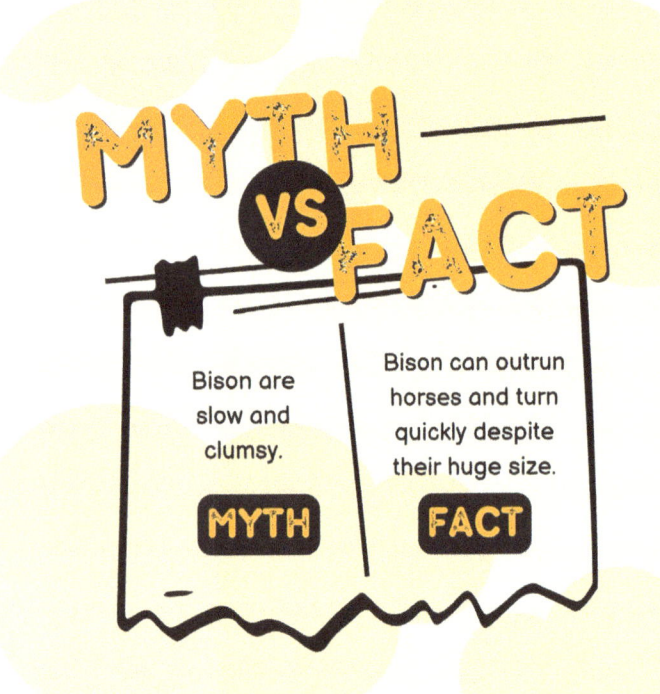

Communication in bison herds involves various sounds and body language. Bulls make deep grunting sounds during mating season, while cows and calves recognize each other's calls in the herd. Bison also use their tails as signals—a raised tail can warn others of danger.

Young bison often play together, chasing each other and practice-fighting, which helps them develop the strength and skills they'll need as adults. Within the herd, bison cooperate to protect each other. When danger approaches, adults form a circle around the calves to protect them. During blizzards, herds move together, taking turns breaking trail through deep snow. This teamwork helps bison survive the challenges of life on the prairie.

Fun Fact: Bison have best friends! Scientists have discovered that certain bison prefer to hang out with specific herd members and will seek each other out day after day.

Fun Fact: Bison are excellent swimmers! They've been spotted crossing rivers over half a mile wide, paddling with their heads and humps bobbing above the water like furry boats.

On the Move

Unlike many animals that are **territorial** and defend a specific area, bison are **migratory** animals. They move across huge areas of land, following the growth of fresh grass and seeking the best conditions throughout the year.

These movements aren't random wandering—bison follow traditional routes that have been used for generations. In spring, they follow the growth of new grass northward. During summer, they spread out across the prairies where grass is plentiful. As winter approaches, they move to areas that offer better protection from harsh weather and where grass remains accessible despite snow.

Before fences and roads divided the prairie, bison made some of the longest land migrations in North America. Today while most bison live in protected areas with more limited range, some herds still make seasonal movements within their available habitat. In places like Yellowstone National Park, bison continue to move between summer and winter ranges, traveling up and down mountain slopes as the seasons change.

Bison communicate their presence to other herds through various signs. They create wallows—shallow depressions in the ground created by rolling and dust bathing—which serve as markers and meeting places. Bulls also leave scent marks and make deep grunting sounds during mating season to advertise their presence.

A Day in the Life

Bison are most active during dawn and dusk, though they can be seen feeding at any time of day or night. Like many grazing animals, they prefer to feed during the cooler hours when the sun isn't too strong.

A typical day for a bison begins at dawn. Herds spend several hours grazing, moving slowly across the prairie as they feed. During the hottest part of the day, especially in summer, bison often rest. During these breaks, they might take dust baths in shallow depressions called wallows, which helps keep biting insects away and cools them off.

When resting, bison often lie down to chew their cud—partially digested grass that they bring back up to chew again. Unlike many animals that seek shelter to rest, bison usually stay out in the open where they can easily spot danger. They may doze while resting but remain alert to their surroundings.

In late afternoon, bison become active again, grazing until dusk. They continue to feed and move throughout the night, though they're generally less active than during daylight hours.

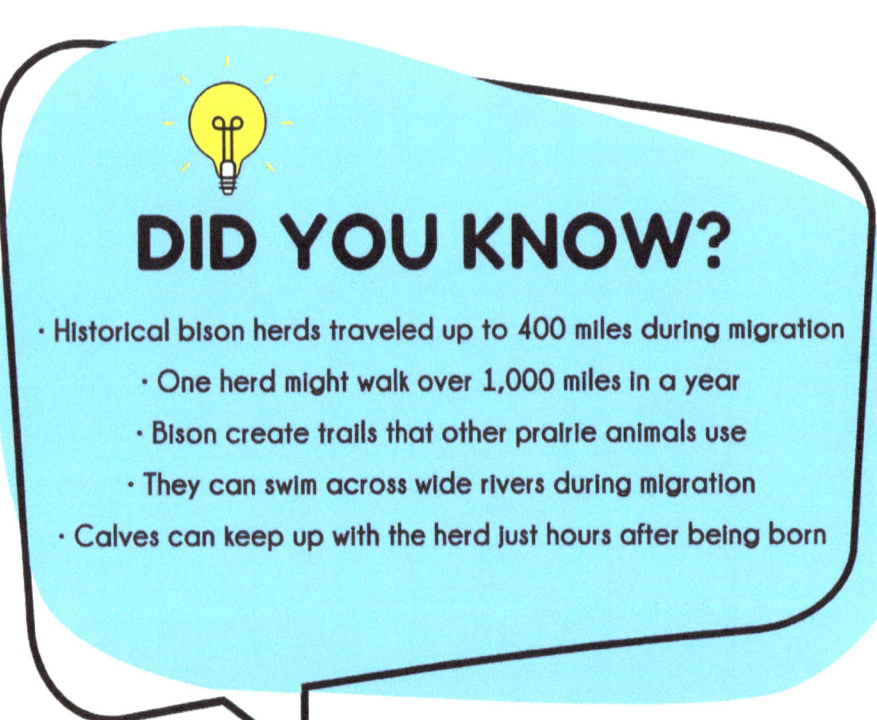

DID YOU KNOW?
- Historical bison herds traveled up to 400 miles during migration
- One herd might walk over 1,000 miles in a year
- Bison create trails that other prairie animals use
- They can swim across wide rivers during migration
- Calves can keep up with the herd just hours after being born

Young bison are especially active, often running, bucking, and play-fighting, which are important for their development and integration into the herd's social structure.

Fun Fact: Bison wallows can last for decades! Some depressions in Yellowstone have been used by bison for over 100 years, passed down through generations like family swimming pools.

Mating and Birth

During breeding season, called the rut, male bison (bulls) compete for the chance to mate with multiple females. The rut occurs from July to September. During this time, adult bulls join the female herds and display their strength through behaviors like bellowing—making deep grunting sounds that can be heard from far away—and fighting with other males.

During the rut, bulls become more aggressive as they compete for females. They may charge at each other, clash heads, or engage in pushing contests. These battles help determine which bulls will have the opportunity to mate. Despite their fierce competitions, serious injuries are rare.

Female bison (cows) usually give birth to one calf after a pregnancy of about 9 to 9.5 months. Most calves are born in spring, typically April or May, when grass is abundant and weather is mild. A newborn calf weighs between 30 to 70 pounds (14 to 32 kg). Twin calves are extremely rare.

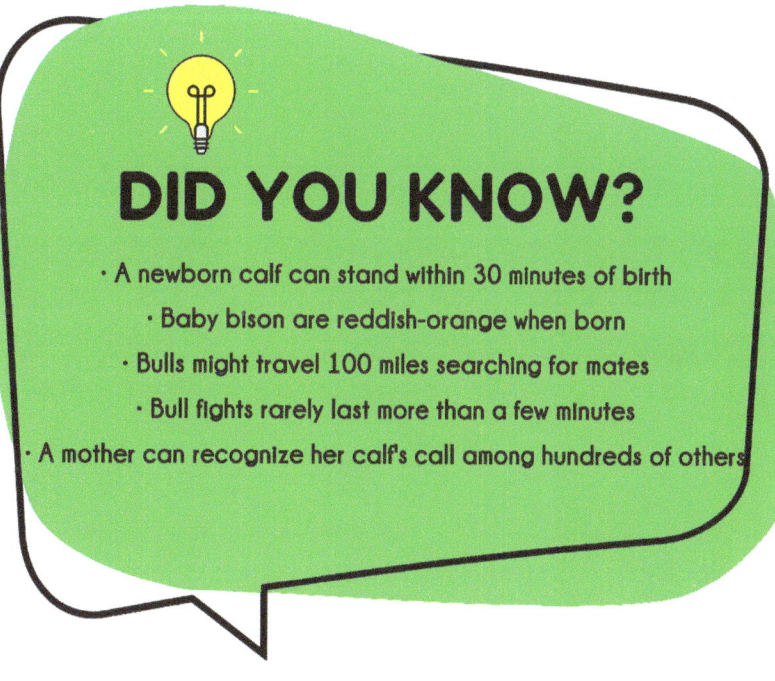

DID YOU KNOW?
- A newborn calf can stand within 30 minutes of birth
- Baby bison are reddish-orange when born
- Bulls might travel 100 miles searching for mates
- Bull fights rarely last more than a few minutes
- A mother can recognize her calf's call among hundreds of others

Females usually have one calf every year or every other year, depending on their health and environmental conditions. The timing of births in spring is important because it gives calves the best chance of survival—they have several months to grow strong before facing their first winter.

Growing Up Bison

Bison calves are nature's quick starters—they can stand and walk within hours of being born. This quick development is crucial for survival—calves need to be able to keep up with the herd almost immediately. Despite being able to walk so soon, calves still depend heavily on their mothers for protection, warmth, and milk.

Bison mothers are very protective of their calves, keeping them close and defending them fiercely from any threats. A calf will stay near its mother for the first year of life, nursing for 7-8 months before switching completely to grass. During this time, the mother teaches her calf essential survival skills, like what plants to eat and how to survive harsh weather.

Bison mothers are the primary caregivers for their calves, but other members of the herd, particularly other females, may help with looking after the young. This communal care includes monitoring the calves and sometimes protecting them, which not only assists the mother but also helps maintain the cohesive social structure of the herd.

Young bison learn important social skills by playing with other calves in the herd. They chase each other, practice fighting, and learn how to behave as part of the herd. As they grow older, young males gradually spend more time at the edges of the herd. By age two or three, young bulls usually leave to join bachelor groups of other males, while young females typically stay with their birth herd.

Fun Fact: Bison are gardeners without knowing it! Seeds that pass through their digestive system often sprout better than seeds that don't—bison basically plant flowers wherever they poop!

Bison and Their Ecosystem

Bison are an integral part of their prairie **ecosystems** in several important ways:

- **Grass Management:** Bison grazing helps maintain prairie grasslands. Their selective feeding prevents any one type of grass from becoming too dominant, which helps maintain plant diversity. The way they graze also stimulates new grass growth, making the prairie more productive.

- **Prairie Engineering:** As bison move and feed, they create wallows—shallow depressions made by rolling and dust bathing. These wallows collect water when it rains, creating mini-wetlands that support unique plants and provide homes for prairie animals like toads and insects.

- **Nutrient Cycling:** Bison droppings fertilize the soil and help spread grass seeds across the prairie. Their hooves break up soil and press seeds into the ground, helping new plants grow.

- **Supporting Other Species:** Bison have **symbiotic** relationships with various species, including birds that feed on the insects stirred up by bison as they move or those that pick parasites from bison fur. These interactions contribute to the health and balance of the ecosystem.

- **Shaping the Landscape:** Bison trails create natural firebreaks that help control prairie fires. Their grazing patterns also help prevent trees from taking over grasslands, maintaining the open habitat that many prairie species need.

- **Indicator Species:** Bison populations reflect the overall health of prairie ecosystems. Changes in their populations can indicate shifts in environmental health and are used to assess the impact of environmental changes.

- **Conservation Symbol:** Historically near extinction, the recovery of bison populations has become a flagship effort in North American conservation, symbolizing the potential for successful restoration of native species and their habitats.

By focusing on protecting bison and the vast prairies they inhabit, conservationists not only ensure the survival of this iconic species but also the health and diversity of the entire grassland ecosystem.

Natural Predators

Adult bison have few natural predators thanks to their massive size and strength. Only wolves and grizzly bears pose a threat, and these predators typically target calves, old, or sick bison rather than healthy adults. A bison calf is most vulnerable in its first few months of life before it grows large enough to defend itself.

Despite their generally peaceful nature, adult bison are well-equipped for defense. They can use their sharp horns and enormous strength to fight off predators. When threatened, the herd works together—adults form a circle around calves, facing outward to confront the danger. A charging bison can easily drive away most predators.

Before European settlement, when vast herds roamed the continent, bison faced more regular predation from wolves and grizzly bears. Today, such encounters are rare because there are fewer large predators and most bison live in protected areas. Only in places like Yellowstone National Park can you still see the natural relationship between bison and their predators play out as it did for thousands of years.

DID YOU KNOW?

- A charging bison can outrun a horse
- Adult bison are too big for a single wolf to attack
- Grizzly bears mainly hunt young or weak bison
- Bison use their horns and hooves for defense
- The whole herd helps protect young calves

Fun Fact: Wolves in Yellowstone have learned that bison are dangerous—a single kick from a bison can break bones or even kill a wolf. Smart wolf packs test herds carefully before committing to a hunt.

Fun Fact: Some Native American tribes are leading bison conservation today. The InterTribal Buffalo Council works with over 80 tribes to restore bison to tribal lands across the country.

Challenges and Threats

Aside from natural predators, bison face numerous other threats and challenges, many of which are human-related:

- **Habitat Loss:** The vast prairies where bison once roamed have largely been converted to farmland and cities. Today, most wild bison live in protected areas like national parks, but these spaces are much smaller than their historical range. This loss of habitat makes it difficult for bison herds to access the large areas they need for grazing, mating, and migration, impacting their ability to maintain healthy populations.

- **Disease:** Bison are susceptible to various diseases, which can spread quickly through herds and have devastating effects. Diseases like brucellosis and tuberculosis, some of which can also be transmitted to livestock, pose significant management challenges, especially where bison and cattle coexist.

- **Climate Change:** Rising temperatures and changing rainfall patterns affect the grasslands where bison live. Droughts can reduce the amount of grass available for food, while severe winters can make it harder for bison to survive.

- **Human-Wildlife Conflict:** As bison habitat overlaps with agricultural lands, there are increased risks of conflicts. Bison may damage crops, fencing, and property as they migrate and forage, leading to tensions with landowners and farmers.

Conservation efforts are vital to mitigate these threats and ensure the survival of bison populations. Initiatives such as habitat restoration, legal protections, managed breeding programs, disease management, and conflict resolution strategies are being implemented to support bison recovery and sustainability. These efforts not only help preserve bison but also the prairie ecosystems they support, maintaining biodiversity and ecological health.

Life Span and Population

In the wild, bison typically live 15 to 20 years. In protected settings like national parks and preserves, where they receive veterinary care and have reliable food sources, bison can live up to 30-40 years.

Bison are an incredible conservation success story. In the late 1800s, these magnificent animals were nearly driven to extinction, with fewer than 1,000 remaining from herds that once numbered in the millions. Through dedicated conservation efforts, bison populations have rebounded. Today, there are about 500,000 bison in North America, though only around 30,000 are managed for conservation in wild or semi-wild herds. The rest live on private ranches where they are raised for meat.

Bison Comeback

- 1500s: 30–60 million bison
- 1889: Fewer than 1,000 bison left
- 1905: First bison protection laws
- 1960s: Herds slowly growing
- Today: About 500,000 bison in North America

Most wild bison today live in protected areas like Yellowstone National Park, which has one of the largest wild herds with about 5,000 animals. Other significant herds can be found in Badlands National Park, Wind Cave National Park, and various national wildlife refuges and tribal lands across North America.

While bison numbers have grown significantly from their lowest point, they still occupy only a tiny fraction of their historical range. Continued conservation efforts focus on maintaining genetic diversity in existing herds and finding new areas where wild bison can roam freely.

Fun Fact: You can visit wild bison at more than 20 national parks and wildlife refuges across North America. Yellowstone's herd has never been fenced in—they're truly wild!

Conclusion

Bison are truly majestic and awe-inspiring creatures. Their powerful presence, social structures, and the role they play in North American prairies teach us about the importance of resilience, community, and the delicate balance of ecosystems.

However, the future is not entirely secure for bison. It's essential for us to recognize the numerous threats they face, including habitat loss, disease, and conflicts with human interests, and to work towards protecting bison and the vast landscapes they live in.

While we can't bring back the large herds that once roamed across North America, today's recovering bison populations show what we can achieve through dedicated conservation efforts. Working together we can protect existing herds and find new areas where bison can roam freely.

Thanks to these efforts, more people than ever can see wild bison in national parks and preserves. These living links to North America's past help us understand what the continent was like when millions of bison shaped the prairie landscape. They remind us that every animal plays an important role in nature's balance.

The bison's recovery teaches us that when people work together to protect nature, we can make a real difference. While challenges remain, the return of bison to parts of their former range gives us hope for the future. By continuing to protect these magnificent animals and the grasslands they call home, we can ensure that future generations will share their world with wild bison.

Test Your Bison Knowledge!

Think you remember everything about these mighty prairie giants? See how many questions you can answer!

🐃 1. What is the scientific name for the American bison?
A) Bovus americanus B) Bison bison C) Buffalo bison D) Bos taurus

🐃 2. True or False: Both male and female bison have horns.

🐃 3. How fast can a bison run?
A) 15 mph B) 25 mph C) 35 mph D) 50 mph

🐃 4. What is a male bison called?
A) Buck B) Bull C) Stallion D) Ram

🐃 5. What color are baby bison when they're born?
A) Dark brown B) Black C) Reddish-orange D) Gray

🐃 6. What is the large hump on a bison's shoulders made of?
A) Fat B) Bone C) Muscle D) Air pockets

🐃 7. How much grass can an adult bison eat per day?
A) 5 pounds B) 15 pounds C) 30 pounds D) 50 pounds

🐃 8. What shallow depressions do bison create by rolling in the dirt?
A) Burrows B) Wallows C) Dens D) Craters

🐃 9. About how many bison were left in North America by the late 1800s?
A) Fewer than 1,000 B) About 10,000 C) Around 100,000 D) Over 1 million

🐃 10. Where can you find the largest wild bison herd in the United States today?
A) Grand Canyon B) Yellowstone National Park C) Central Park D) Everglades

Answer Key: 1-B, 2-True, 3-C, 4-B, 5-C, 6-C, 7-C, 8-B, 9-A, 10-B

STEM Challenge: Think Like a Scientist!

Bison are built to survive blazing summers and freezing winters on the open prairie. Try these hands-on experiments to discover how their adaptations help them thrive!

Snowplow Power

Topic: Physics & Engineering

You'll Need:
Shallow baking pan, flour or sand, wooden spoon, small toy shovel, timer

What to Do:
1. Fill the pan with 2 inches of flour or sand (this is your "snow")
2. Use the toy shovel to clear a path by pushing forward—time how long it takes
3. Now use the back of the wooden spoon, sweeping side to side like a bison's head
4. Which method cleared the path faster?

What You'll Learn:
Bison sweep their massive heads side to side to clear snow and reach buried grass. Their powerful neck muscles and heavy skull work like a built-in snowplow—no digging required!

Hollow Hair Insulation Test

Topic: Adaptation & Heat Transfer

You'll Need:
2 jars with lids, hot water, 2 thermometers, drinking straws (cut into 1-inch pieces), cotton balls, rubber bands, timer

What to Do:
1. Wrap one jar with cotton balls and secure with rubber bands (regular fur)
2. Wrap the other jar with cut straw pieces arranged pointing outward, then cover with a thin layer of cotton (hollow hair fur)
3. Fill both jars with equally hot water and seal the lids
4. Check the temperature every 5 minutes for 20 minutes
5. Which jar stayed warmer longer?

What You'll Learn:
Bison fur has two layers—a woolly undercoat plus longer hollow guard hairs that trap air. Air is a great insulator! This double layer keeps bison warm in temperatures far below freezing.

Word Search

```
P B M X M I Q P M I G R A T E
L R R C H C Q D S W O L L A W
V S E V O O H G M Y X W C R P
V C E D C W F L E G Y X Y P F
L A M C A E S T T A R W M V E
B Y A Y Y T G C S Y O A D Q E
B S M V E F O G Y B I Z S T J
M E M F L Z L R S O D J A S D
N I A T L V U D O D H M O M Z
Z C L C O T Y M C A I E E B A
Q E S W W S P C E L R E K T H
X P N B S N G S C O C U D D O
G S C I T R F R V R V F R X S
L I G S O O X I A I M E W O R
F D F O N H B X W Z H K Z C U
L D H N E R N T A T I B A H A
A X P H E Q B U L L S N B R T
C D X H P R A I R I E S G P V
```

BISON	GRASS	MAMMALS
BULLS	GRAZING	MIGRATE
CALF	HABITAT	PRAIRIES
CLIMATE	HERBIVORE	PREDATOR
COWS	HERD	SPECIES
CUD	HOOVES	WALLOWS
ECOSYSTEM	HORNS	YELLOWSTONE

Glossary

adaptations – special features or behaviors that help a plant or animal survive in its environment

ecosystem – a community of living things and their environment, all connected and depending on each other

habitat – the natural home or environment where a plant or animal lives

herbivores – animals that eat only plants

mammals – warm-blooded animals that have hair or fur and feed their babies with milk from the mother

migratory – moving from one place to another, usually with the seasons

predators – animals that hunt other animals for food

regurgitate – to bring food back up from the stomach to chew it again

rut – the breeding season when male bison compete for mates

symbiotic – when different living things help each other out in nature

territorial – defending a certain area as one's own space

vertebrae – the series of small bones that make up the backbone

Resources and References

Want to learn more about bison? Check out these great resources!

Books

American Bison: A Natural History by Dale F. Lott – A detailed look at bison biology and behavior.

The Time of the Buffalo by Tom McHugh – The history of bison in North America.

Websites

National Geographic Kids – American Bison
www.nationalgeographic.com/animals/mammals/facts/american-bison
Explore photos, videos, and fun facts about bison and their prairie home.

Yellowstone National Park – Bison
www.nps.gov/yell/learn/nature/bison.htm
Learn about the largest wild bison herd in the United States and efforts to protect them.

World Wildlife Fund – Plains Bison
www.worldwildlife.org/species/plains-bison
Discover how conservationists are working to bring bison back to their native lands.

Smithsonian National Zoo – American Bison
nationalzoo.si.edu/animals/american-bison
Meet the bison at the Smithsonian and learn about their behavior and biology.

The Nature Conservancy – Restoring the Great Plains Bison
www.nature.org/en-us/what-we-do/our-priorities/protect-water-and-land/land-and-water-stories/american-bison-conservation/
See how bison are being returned to prairies across North America.

Places to See Bison

Yellowstone National Park (Wyoming, Montana, Idaho), Badlands National Park (South Dakota), Wind Cave National Park (South Dakota), Theodore Roosevelt National Park (North Dakota), Tallgrass Prairie National Preserve (Kansas), National Bison Range (Montana)

Keep Exploring!

If you enjoyed learning about bison, explore other titles in the *This Incredible Planet* series to discover more amazing animals—from sea turtles to penguins to elephants—and the habitats they call home.

Index

A
adaptations, 12

B
birth, 23
breeding, 23
bulls, 16, 23

C
calves, 23, 24
challenges, 31
climate change, 31
coat, 12
communication, 16, 19
conservation, 7, 27, 31, 32
cows, 16, 23
cud, 20

D
daily life, 20
defenses, 28
diet, 15
digestive system, 12, 15
disease, 31

E
ecosystem, 27
environment, 11

F
firebreaks, 27
fur, 12

G
grasslands, 11, 27
grizzly bears, 28

H
habitat, 11
habitat loss, 31
head, 12
herbivores, 15
herds, 16, 24
hide, 12
hooves, 12
horns, 8
human-wildlife conflict, 31

I
indicator species, 27

L

lifespan, 32

M
mating, 23
migration, 18–19, 20
mothers, 23, 24

N
national parks, 31, 32
neck, 12
nutrient cycling, 27

P
parenting, 24
physical adaptations, 12
physical appearance, 7, 8, 12
population, 7, 32
predators, 28

R
reproduction, 23
rut, 23

S
scientific name, 7
seasons, 11, 15, 16, 19
senses, 12
shoulder hump, 12
size, 8
sleep, 20
social behavior, 16
speed, 11
symbiotic relationships, 27

T
territory, 18
threats, 31

W
wallows, 21, 27
wolves, 28, 29

www.ingramcontent.com/pod-product-compliance
Lightning Source LLC
Chambersburg PA
CBHW040224040426
42333CB00051B/3433